Cecilia Whitford

JAPANESE PRINTS

With 41 colour plates

THAMES AND HUDSON · LONDON

First published in the UK in 1977 by
Thames and Hudson Ltd, London

© Blacker Calmann Cooper Ltd, 1977
This book was designed and produced by
Blacker Calmann Cooper Ltd, London

Filmset by Brown Knight and Truscott Ltd, Tonbridge, Kent
Printed in Spain by Heraclio Fournier, S.A.

Introduction

'IT IS NOT TOO MUCH TO SAY that no event in the artistic world has of late years attracted so much attention as the discovery of the wonderful skill in painting possessed by the people of that strange empire in the Western Pacific.'

This large claim was made by an anonymous writer in *Blackwood's Magazine* in February 1887 who was referring, of course, to the art of Japan. The claim was large, but could easily be justified. For ever since the 1850s, when Japan had emerged from two centuries of almost total, self-imposed isolation, her art and artefacts had thrilled Europe and America with their strange beauty and amazing technical skill.

The vogue for Japan and its art was at its height when the *Blackwood's* article was written. It had, as all vogues must, its ridiculous side; but it also exerted a powerful, far-reaching influence on the greatest artists of the period: on Manet, Degas, the Impressionists, van Gogh, Gauguin and Toulouse-Lautrec. They admired and collected all kinds of Japanese art, but reserved their greatest admiration for the polychromatic wood-block prints that were exported to Europe in huge quantities and sold at prices that even impecunious painters like van Gogh could afford. Such European artists loved Japanese prints for their bright, clear colours, for their sense of decorative balance and for their exotic subjects. Without much accurate knowledge of Japan itself, the European painters often misunderstood the significance of the subject-matter and were not concerned by the historical and social pressures which had caused the flowering of the Japanese print.

During the sixteenth century in Japan, long-standing wars of rivalry between the feudal lords came to an end and the country was unified. As a result of the peace, and of the unification, the traditional arts experienced a renaissance. The military class, the *samurai*, began to beautify their castles, which, until then, had been little more than forbidding fortresses. Painters and sculptors were commissioned to decorate sliding doors, ceilings and wood panels, weavers and seamstresses to produce extravagantly beautiful clothes. Every form of art and craft was vitalized by the desire of the powerful *samurai* to make their lives as luxurious as possible.

The great merchant families of the cities of Kyoto and Sakai, whose money had provided the *samurai* with guns and ammunition, also wanted to improve the quality of their lives. Since they were of a lower social order than the military, the merchants did not pretend to the aristocratic forms of art, nor to high culture. They commissioned paintings depicting pretty courtesans, visited the new *Kabuki* dances and read popular books that were lavishly illustrated by hand. Some of these story books were produced as scrolls, some were bound. The demand for these illustrated manuscripts, however, became so great that they could no longer be made by hand. Thus, the picture-book printed from cut wood blocks was born.

Although the technique of printing from wood blocks had been known in Japan for many centuries, and although Chinese printed books were quite common, the first Japanese illustrated book printed from wood blocks did not appear until around 1650; it was the *Ise Monogatari*, a traditional tale. The illustrations in such early printed books were crude and subordinate to the text. Very soon, however, the pictures became more important and, crude though they were, provided the masses with a cheap form of art. Even illiterates bought books for the sake of the pictures.

Around 1660 there were many illustrators working under contract for publishers in Japan's most important city, Edo, present-day Tokyo. One of them, Hishikawa Moronobu, persuaded his publisher to issue illustrations as single sheets and without texts. These sold very well, and from then on, wood-block prints as well as illustrated books were freely available. Moronobu must have been aware that his single prints were the start of something important. He not only signed each print in the wood block, but his signature announced to the world that he took himself seriously as an artist. It was *Yamato eshi* – master of Japanese painting.

Japanese prints are often referred to as *ukiyo-e*. The word *ukiyo* was originally Buddhist and meant 'sad world'. By the seventeenth century, however, the word had come to mean 'floating world': a world of transient pleasures, free from care. The prints and paintings that the merchants commissioned and bought almost always depicted aspects of a carefree existence, and were therefore called *ukiyo-e*: pictures of the floating world. To understand the prints, we must understand something of the *ukiyo*, or at least those aspects of it which the print-makers were especially fond of depicting: the theatre, life in the pleasure quarters, and travel.

By the sixteenth century, the *Nō* drama had become the preserve of the aristocracy and the higher ranks of the military. The lower social orders were permitted only to attend some of the dances associated with the *No* drama. The popular *Kabuki* theatre, which provided the print-makers with so many of their subjects, developed out of these dances.

Around the middle of the sixteenth century, a troupe of entertainers, led by a woman, became popular in Kyoto. It specialized in dances performed by men masquerading as women, and women as men. Many such troupes soon emerged, some of which consisted only of women who were less interested in dancing than in offering their sexual services for sale. The authorities soon prohibited them. The girls were then replaced by boys who, in turn, were also banned for the same reason. Finally, adult males took over, and they began to liven up the performances by acting out some of the popular stories of the day. The result was the form of the *Kabuki* theatre that has endured, with little modification, until today.

In contemporary slang, *kabuku* meant 'fashionable', and it is thought that the name *Kabuki* developed from it. The theatre was not only fashionable, it was also very popular, partly because it was the only outside entertainment to which respectable women might go. Not only the leisured wives and daughters of the merchants flocked to the theatre but also, on their few free days, the ladies of the court. Some of these women were fortunate, or forward enough to have actors as lovers, but most of them had to be content with portrait-prints of their favourites. Publishers were aware of this demand, and commissioned artists to depict every aspect of the life of the actor and the *Kabuki* theatre. They showed actors relaxing backstage, holding a dramatic pose or out walking. They also produced single and group portraits. The theatre provided the print-makers with an inexhaustible supply of subjects, and the prints boosted the popularity of the actors and of particular plays.

There were, of course, as many male enthusiasts of the *Kabuki* as there were female devotees. For the men, however, there was a more important place of entertainment: the brothel. The craftsmen and merchants possessed enough money and time to allow them to live large parts of their lives with courtesans and prostitutes, and a large industry grew up to meet their needs. By 1617, all the whores and brothels in Edo had been concentrated in one place, called the

Yoshiwara, and were licensed for prostitution. After a disastrous fire in 1657, which virtually destroyed Edo and caused the city to be replanned and rebuilt, another district was specially cleared for prostitution and called the New Yoshiwara, which continued in its specialized trade until 1951. Other important cities also had their licensed districts, and both the government and the licensees did their best to suppress illegal premises and independent prostitutes, but with varying success.

For the average Japanese man of the period, the brothel was not just a place for extramarital sex. The Yoshiwara and the unlicensed quarters provided relaxation and entertainment of all kinds. Its purpose was to give the customer a good time – at a price. The degradation of women in bondage, the blandishments of both buyer and seller were, of course, immediately beneath the seductive veneer, and everybody knew it; but the Yoshiwara was also a place where a poor girl, if she were clever and lucky, could be bought out by some rich suitor, possibly even a feudal lord, and where a rich merchant could enjoy the power provided by his money. In the Yoshiwara, the impecunious *samurai* received the minimum service while his social inferior, the wealthy merchant, was treated like the *samurai's* lord.

The most accomplished courtesans provided the print-makers with many of their subjects. Although prints of explicit sexual activity were popular, the courtesan was as frequently depicted showing off her extravagant kimonos like a fashion model, demonstrating the latest hairstyle and enjoying her allegedly leisured way of life. She was a star, and her portrait, bought by admirers and by those who wished they could afford her, increased the demand for her and the profits of her house.

Once Hishikawa Moronobu had signed his prints and had called himself a master, other artists followed his example and, in true Japanese fashion, master-pupil relationships developed. Schools of print-making, each with its preferred subjects and characteristic style, emerged. They were known as families because the head pupil often married into his master's family and established a true blood relationship. In the early eighteenth century families such as the Hishikawa (Moronobu's followers), the Torii (who specialized in actor-prints) and the Kaigetsudo (masters of full-length prints of beautiful women) were especially prominent.

The early eighteenth century was a period of development in print-making. The quality of paper improved; shapes and sizes of prints became varied; and polyptychs were introduced. Techniques of printing became more sophisticated. The *urushi-e*, or lacquer-print was developed, for example, in which certain areas of black are made to shine by mixing glue with the printing-ink.

The greatest innovation in technique, however, was in the use of colour. From the earliest times, de-luxe editions of prints had been richly coloured by hand, and by the middle of the eighteenth century Okumura Masanobu (a publisher as well as an artist) was experimenting with the use of more than one block to produce *beni-e*, or 'red pictures' which employed up to three colours. These colours were not contained by the contours of the design however.

The first truly polychromatic print (called *nishiki-e*, or 'brocade picture' in Japanese) appeared around 1769. An Edo artist, Suzuki Harunobu published a series of prints in which the colours were either enclosed by an outline, or formed hard edges on their own. These prints were an instant success and Harunobu, until his death six years later at the age of 46, was the most popular artist in Edo, producing prints of ethereal, identical-looking young men and women, posing with exquisite grace.

Students of printing techniques marvel at the way in which the Japanese managed to produce such fine work in so many colours with wood, a most unwieldy material. What makes Japanese wood-block prints radically different from their Western counterparts, is that they were the combined production of a team, and not of one artist. The publisher commissioned the designer with a specific project; then the cutters went to work on the design; the inkers and printers produced it, and the prints were sold from the publisher's shops and by street hawkers.

The designer produced a drawing on thin paper in black ink. This drawing was stuck down on a block of, usually, pear or cherry wood, which was cut with the grain. The cutting was done with tools very like their Western equivalents; however, the actual printing was done very differently as no press was used. First, the colour was brushed on to the block, using a water-soluble pigment. The paper was placed on the block, and its back was rubbed over with a small, smooth, circular tool, called a *baren*. By careful and clever brushing, and by calculated changes in pressure and direction of the *baren*, extremely subtle colour variations could be achieved. The first colour was usually black, and this established the outlines. Proofs of the first block were then used to make further blocks – one for each colour – using the same methods. At the height of the print-making tradition, it was not unusual for prints to include fifteen different colours. Blind-stamping, lacquer and other special effects made them still more dazzling.

With the appearance of the brocade picture, the *nishiki-e*, began the golden age of print-making. This period lasted only for about forty years, but it witnessed the technical perfection of print-making, and benefitted from the unusually large number of superior talents then at work. By the time of Harunobu's death, another brilliant artist had begun to dominate the market. This was Torii Kiyonaga. Although Kiyonaga was the head of the family which specialized in actor-prints, he did not design any himself – out of deference, it is said, to the true heir, who was only a child at the time. Instead, he depicted unusual aspects of the theatre: scenes backstage, for example, or the chorus of a play rather than its main protagonists. He is best remembered for *bijin-ga*, pictures of beautiful women, who are tall, elegant, handsome creatures, often shown in large groups or placed across the several sheets of a polyptych and wearing exquisite clothes against an intricate background. Kiyonaga was said to make his publishers weep because his designs could only be cut by the most skilled and consequently the most expensive craftsmen.

Kitagawa Utamaro, whose *bijin-ga* are probably the most famous pictures of beautiful women in all of Japanese print-making, was a younger contemporary of Kiyonaga. He was discovered by Tatsuya Juzaburo, a wealthy publisher, who also wrote and designed prints in his spare time. Utamaro was told to compete with Kiyonaga and to make superior prints of women. This he did, and in a period in which great talent was commonplace, Utamaro managed to stay on top almost until his death. He was not, however, only a painter of women. The work which established his reputation was a book of poems called *Ehon mushi erami*, which was lavishly illustrated with pictures of insects, reptiles and plants.

In 1794 an artist appeared on the scene with prints of actors, the like of which no-one had ever seen before. They were not conventional portraits, but often cruel caricatures of the most popular actors of the day. Ten months later, the artist had ceased to work and was not heard of again. This was Toshusai Sharaku, the greatest mystery, and one of the greatest designers, in the history of print making. No one knows why his career was so brief.

Perhaps his work annoyed publishers and actors; perhaps he simply died.

During the first half of the nineteenth century print-makers continued to use traditional subjects, but the public was gradually changing. A growing feeling of claustrophobia, in a country closed to the outside world, produced the desire to know as much as possible of what lay beyond the seas, and of Japan itself; but there was also a growing demand for sensational prints depicting the grotesque and the sadistic. In spite of the wish for new subjects, a new family specializing in theatrical prints emerged during the nineteenth century. This was the Utagawa family, whose distinguished members included Toyokuni, Kunisada and Kuniyoshi. Kunisada (also known as Toyokuni III) was probably the most prolific print designer in history. His repertoire included not only actors and women, but also landscape prints and erotica. Because he produced so much, Kunisada's work is often mediocre; but at his best, he ranks with the greatest masters.

The growing desire for landscape prints was satisfied in brilliant fashion by Katsushika Hokusai and Ando Hiroshige, who are probably the best-known print-artists in the West. They were the last truly great designers in the history of Japanese print-making. Hokusai was ninety years old when he died in 1849, and his career had therefore begun during the golden age of print-making. According to his autobiography, he began to draw at the age of six; he thought he had finally achieved some insight at the age of seventy-three and he hoped that he would have achieved complete mastery by the time he was one hundred and ten. He was a perfectionist of the most troublesome kind: uncompromising, stubborn, a trial to all he worked with. He illustrated and sometimes wrote novels, and his erotic work is often frighteningly sensational, but his many landscapes most clearly demonstrate his genius for description and for the evocation of atmosphere. Hokusai was almost always in demand but almost always in trouble with his publishers. One of his many signatures is *Gakyojin*, the madman of painting: he knew himself well.

Around 1822 Hokusai produced what he thought was his masterpiece: the series *Thirty-six Views of Mount Fuji*, which includes the well-known *Red Fuji*, *Fuji by Lightning* and, perhaps the most famous of all Japanese prints, *The Great Wave*. While the series was in production, an artist thirty-six years Hokusai's junior began selling a rival series from a rival house, much to Hokusai's consternation. This was Ando Hiroshige, and his series of landscapes, the *Fifty-three Stations of the Tokaido* became an instant success.

Hokusai immediately countered with a book containing a further series of views of Mount Fuji in black and white. Although this book was also a success, the buying public decided the result of the contest – they preferred the gentler, more sentimental attitude to landscape that Hiroshige offered to the more mannered style of Hokusai. Both Hiroshige and Hokusai were fervently admired by French artists in the nineteenth century, and aspects of their landscape technique inspired both the Impressionists and Post-Impressionists such as van Gogh and Gauguin.

After Japan had emerged from the long period of isolation from the rest of the world, it became swamped with Western technology of all kinds which threatened to eliminate all traditional forms of Japanese life. Tradition survived in many areas, but the wood-block print, unequal to the challenge of photography, was not one of them.

The print was a long time dying, however, and its eventual demise was not without dignity. The print-makers became journalists, describing life in other countries and depicting the enormous changes brought about by the contact with the West. They showed Edo, now called Tokyo, being rebuilt in European fashion and chronicled the introduction of railways, steam ships, modern industrial machinery and Western styles of dress and behaviour. An unexpected boom in print-making came with the declaration of the Sino-Japanese war in 1894. Many artists produced hundreds of prints, entirely from their imagination, of the triumphant progress of the Japanese army. These were cut and printed in a matter of hours and sold to a delighted public. Most of these prints are of dubious quality, but they continued the tradition of those artists who sat in the front row of the *Kabuki* theatre, ready to capture a dramatic moment in the play for a print that would be in the shops on the following day.

In the present century there have been many attempts to revive the art of print-making in Japan; these have almost always failed because they have been made by artists who self-consciously see themselves as reviving a tradition and who regard what they are doing as high art. The greatest prints were not produced as high art, but were frankly popular, commercial and expendable, which is why the Japanese themselves could not regard Japanese wood-block prints as great artistic creations until the Europeans had taught them to. It is also why the most comprehensive collections of Japanese prints are today to be found, not in Japan, but in Europe and America, whose artists have benefitted so much from their example.

MORONOBU (*c.*1655–1700)

1. *Riverboat party*

7 × 7¾in (18 × 20cm)

This is a luxury hand-coloured print and shows two young men playing a game of *go*, watched by a woman and a *samurai*. The boatman reclines on the roof of the boat, smoking his pipe. On the right can be seen a *samisen*, the main musical instrument of the *geisha*, entertainers who could be either male or female at this period. *Geisha* came to be in demand in the middle of the eighteenth century when the Yoshiwara courtesans had lost their previous accomplishments and were expected to look after their clients in only the most obvious way.

London, British Museum (1915–8–23–04)

2. Anonymous

c.1700. 6½ × 9½ in (16·5 × 24cm)

The very late date of the completion of this manuscript would indicate that even after printed books appeared, customers who could afford them preferred the colourfully illustrated *Nara ehon* (hand-illustrated books). The *Taketori monogatari*, the oldest known tale in Japanese literature, tells the story of a moon-maiden who is banished to earth, and is wooed by five noblemen and the emperor himself; eventually she has to leave them all and return to the moon. The illustration shows the Shining Princess confronting one of her suitors with a riddle. The pretty colours and the liberal use of gold paint suggests that this is a luxury edition, but the drawing is cruder than that of the print below.

Anonymous

1660. 9 × 6¾ in (23 × 17cm)

The *Utsubo monogatari* was a traditional tale, probably written down in the ninth century. It is a collection of stories revolving around two main plots. This edition covers the first of twenty chapters which deal with the birth in obscurity of one of the heroes and his subsequent adoption by a great noble. The illustration appears to be of his birth, with his mother surrounded by attendants and her old nurse boiling water outside. Since the story has it that she was attended only by her nurse, the anonymous illustrator seems to be treating the subject rather freely. The mother-to-be has the traditional flowing hair-style of a mediaeval *Heian* court lady, but the appearance of the other women is contemporary.

Cambridge, University Library

夏よりたやの乳のゆす母わやしゝしりてる
どすこふいにちハのるゆぬたるねのめぐろ〳〵
もあ〳〵どゝしと抽くゝゝどちとさのゝゝびうりゝ
やんといたふぬろ今ハなふせなふとそのは
なりぬろ御祖ま丙ふ丹すてくゝひきゝ〳〵ゑる
めのやふふゝ城ぬゝいゝるまゝにいとゝふる
さう川ふ〳〵ぞゝすり八さゝんやゝつゝ丙ゝゝよ
三子丹丙こゝゝやのゝく〳〵ゝ丙ゝとゝゝゝろゝる
〳〵

KIYOMASU II (1706–63)

3. *Actor as courtesan holding a wig*

c.1730. 5½ × 11½in (14 × 29cm)

Kiyomasu was a not particularly imaginative member of the Torii family, whose speciality was the actor-print, so it seems likely that the subject of this work is a man playing the part of a courtesan. The actor's stance, with his head turned to one side and his stomach held out, is seen fairly often in early prints, particularly those of the Kaigetsudō school. Why he is holding a wig in his hand is difficult to imagine, but it is interesting to see the hair-styles of this period, which were much less elaborate than they were even ten years later. This type of black and white print, hand-coloured with a distinctive yellow-orange ink, were called *tan-e*.

London, British Museum (1954–4–10–02)

HARUNOBU (1725–70)

4. *Courtesan with her attendant*

10⅞ × 8in (27·5 × 20cm)

A high-ranking courtesan in the Yoshiwara usually had at least one very young apprentice, to be trained by her and to be her personal maid. This system spared the brothel keeper the expense of educating the girl themselves, and even of feeding her as most of the child's meals could be charged to her 'big sister's' clients. The prostitutes of the Yoshiwara tied their wide sashes in front, and always went bare-foot. The large lantern, half hidden behind the pillar, would be carried by a male attendant when the courtesan was summoned to the 'tea house' by a client.

London, British Museum (1915–6–1–03)

HARUNOBU (1725–70)

5. *Osen of the Kagiya serving tea to a customer*

7¾ × 9½in (19·5 × 24cm)

Harunobu was an admirer of Osen, the beautiful proprietress of a famous tea and cake shop called Kagiya, and he depicted her in many of his prints; her customer here, wearing two swords, is a *samurai*. Not only was Harunobu the first *ukiyo-e* artist to portray girls who were not courtesans or *geisha*, but he was also one of the first to use backgrounds in his prints, something that was much copied by his contemporaries. In this print, he has depicted the stone walk leading to a shrine, beside which is one of the pillars of a *torii*, the gate which stands at the entrance of all Shinto shrines.

London, British Museum (1937–7–10–06)

SHUNSHŌ (1726–92)

6. *Two actors arriving backstage*

Before 1785. $14\frac{1}{2} \times 9\frac{7}{8}$ in (37 × 25cm)

Shunshō dominated the field of the actor-print during his
working life, taking it over from the Torii family whose
speciality it had been. He was the first artist to produce
actual portraits of actors; he also drew them in relaxed
surroundings, as in this picture which shows two actors
arriving backstage. The female impersonator is
immediately recognizable by his completely different hair
style and very feminine manner of dress and stance.

London, British Museum (1906–12–20–140)

SHUNSHŌ (1726–92)

7. *Ichikawa Danjūrō V and Segawa Kikunojō*

c.1770. 8¼ × 7in (20 × 18cm)

This print shows a scene from a *kabuki* play which featured the very popular *shitennō*. They were a kind of Japanese Four Musketeers, the faithful followers of another popular historical hero, Minamoto no Raikō. The musketeer here is Sakata no Kintoki, identifiable by the large '*kin*' (the Chinese character for gold) he has on his sleeve, and from his red face. Kintoki as a child and his mother were popular subjects for many print-makers. His mother is supposed to have fled to the mountain when he was a baby, and he grew up, Tarzan-like, with animals as playmates. Whenever print artists felt like depicting a wild woman with flying hair and tattered clothes, they called her Kintoki's mother.

London, British Museum (1906–12–20–137)

SHUNSHŌ (1726–92)

8. *December snow in Nikenjaya*

c.1766. 7¼ × 10¼in (19·5 × 26cm)

The style of this print, from the series *Eight Views of Fukagawa*, shows the strength of Harunobu's influence on his contemporaries. Two *geisha* are entertaining a client, the kneeling girl with the game of stone, scissors and paper. She is the older of the two, her sleeves are shorter, and the colours of her clothes more sombre. Fukagawa was an area of unlicensed brothels which were raided by the police whenever a strict or puritanical administration came to power. It was famous for its *geisha*, girls who at least claimed to be dancers and musicians first and prostitutes second (if at all) Note the *samisen* on the floor. The scenery on the top of the picture shows the local shrine, Tomigaoka Hachiman, framed on two sides by conventionally depicted 'mist'.

London, British Museum (1926–7–14–03)

UTAMARO (1753–1806)

9. *Ehon mushi erami*

1788. 8¾ × 6½in (22 × 16cm)

This print is part of *Ehon mushi erami*, a beautifully
illustrated book on insects, reptiles and flowers; on each
page is a short poem by Ishikawa Masamochi, a popular
writer of the day. When he designed this book, Utamaro
was still under the tutelage of his master, Sekien, whose
most brilliant pupil he was and who wrote a preface to the
book in which he praised Utamaro. The book was
published by Tatsuya Juzaburo, who became Utamaro's
most influential backer. This page shows a locust, an
autumn insect, against a Chinese balloon flower and
pinks, both of which also flower in the autumn.

London, British Museum

UTAMARO (1735–1806)

10. *Games of the Four Seasons: Charms of Flowers*

c.1782. Diptych, each panel 15 × 9¾in (38 × 25cm)

This early work was designed by Utamaro when he was still very conscious of the popularity of Kiyonaga, whose speciality was the composition of groups, especially of standing women. Utamaro, however, has escaped the influence of the older master in the use of colours; his are much brighter and bolder than those of Kiyonaga. He is already using a device for which he became famous – the depiction of gossamer materials; here, a girl is peering through the dress of a standing woman. Since the print is entitled *Games of Four Seasons*, there were probably three other pictures in the set; so far, however, only this one has been found.

London, British Museum (1935–12–010)

UTAMARO (1753–1806)

11. *The hour of the boar*

c.1790. 9½ × 15in (24·5 × 38cm)

This print is from the series, *Twelve hours of the green
houses*, which show Utamaro at his best; the design on the
courtesan's clothes is superb and the filigree cutting
around both girls' hair-lines is fine, but there is no
distracting background and no unnecessary commentary
has been allowed to interfere with the central image. The
courtesan has arrived at the tea-house during the hour of
the boar (9–11 p.m.) with her little attendant. She would
no doubt have been accompanied by an older apprentice,
as well as two or three male servants, who would have
carried a large lantern ahead of her and sometimes even
her bedding. She deigns to attend her client's dinner, but
before she will partake of it, she prepares a large saucer of
warm *sake* and offers it to him. If the client was not used to
the grandiose ceremonies surrounding the purchase of a
prize whore like this one, he could easily become
intimidated; this would be an excuse for the courtesan and
the staff of the tea-house to make him feel even more
inadequate and then to persuade him to spend more
money to mask his insecurity.

London, British Museum (1935–12–14–010)

UTAMARO (1753–1806)

12. *Tsujigimi*

15$\frac{3}{4}$ × 23$\frac{4}{5}$in (40 × 60·5cm)

This picture shows how Utamaro idealized his subjects.
'Tsujigimi' was Osaka slang for the lowest kind of illegal
prostitute, often old and diseased, who plied her trade at
the 'tsuji' or street corner, using a straw mat, which she
carried around with her, on which to lie. This dishevelled,
but young and pretty individual stands with her mat over
the left arm. Her right hand is in her belt, where she
probably keeps her money. There is a comic verse which
tells of one such prostitute who is so cold on a winter
night that she eats two bowls of noodles at 16 *mon* each,
thus prodigally spending the 24 *mon*, her standard price,
which she got from her last client.

London, British Museum (1909–6–18–70)

KIYONAGA (1752–1815)

13. *Kabuki scene with part of the chorus*

10 × 14¼ in (25·5 × 36·5cm)

Kiyonaga was so loyal to the Torii, the family of his master, that he refused to design orthodox actor-prints, which he felt were the special domain of the family heir. Instead, by depicting hitherto ignored aspects of the theatre such as the chorus, he introduced new subjects for print-makers to use. Although the *kabuki* has relatively realistic dialogue, there is a chorus which explains, to a musical accompaniment, the background to the action. This print shows two young lovers leaving the stage, possibly by the 'flower route', a narrow walk to the back of the theatre, passing through the audience. The couple is in the traditional lover's pose: in Japan, a picture of a man and a woman under an umbrella is equivalent to the western heart with an arrow through it.

London, British Museum (1924–7–14–06)

KIYONAGA (1752–1815)

14. *Lessons from the book on behaviour for women*

c.1785. 10½ × 7½in (26·7 × 19cm)

The girl sitting on the ledge is a fully-fledged courtesan.
The other two, with their long, flowing sleeves (which
show them to be unmarried), could be young apprentices,
or perhaps *geisha*, who, in some districts, traditionally
dressed as if they were very much younger than they
were. The series of prints from which this is taken quotes
extracts from an edifying book by a woman on how to
bring up girls. The quotation here ironically advises
against too much play and listening to blind musicians
(story-tellers), the activities enjoyed by the young ladies in
this print.

London, British Museum (1902–2–12–225)

SHARAKU

15. *The actor Ichikawa Komazo II*

1794. 14½ × 9½ in (37 × 24cm)

This is a fine example of the first of the four periods of
Sharaku's short artistic career. In his first period, he
concentrated on the facial characteristics of his actor-
subjects. His disappearance as an artist is sometimes
supposed to be due to the unpopularity of his cruel
caricatures – certainly the actor depicted here would not
wish to be reminded of his big ears and nose, nor would
his fans be pleased with such a portrayal. This is a superb
print, however; note the muted luxury of the steel-grey
mica background, and the economy of colour, which
escapes being dull by the skilful use of the red under the
eyes and the tiny patch near the sword hilt.

London, British Museum (1909-6-18-48)

SHARAKU

16. *The actor Segawa Ichimatsu as Onayo*

1794. 10 × 14¾ in (25·5 × 37·5cm)

This is another example from Sharaku's best period, when he was concentrating on actors' facial expressions. The print has a solid, mica background, better to emphasize the face and the very fine design on the actor's clothes. The cloth Onayo is wearing over the front part of her head is a 'horn-hider' – in Japan, it is the jealous woman (and not the cuckolded husband) who grows the horns.

London, British Museum (1945–11–1–049)

EISHI (1756–1829)

17. *Tomikawa Otami of the Matsubaya*

Before 1800. 9¼ × 14in (23·5 × 35·5cm)

Eishi was an unusual *ukiyo-e* artist, for he was the heir to a respected *samurai* family, had his artistic training in the prestigious Kanō school and was the painting companion to the *Shōgun*, the military governor of the country. He became interested in the wood-block print, resigned from his official position, waived his birthright in favour of his younger brother, and became a print designer. Other *samurai* entered this field before him, but there had always been some bad feeling about it, but in Eishi's case, the transition was effected with hardly any disturbance. Otami was one of the top courtesans of the Matsubaya brothel. Here she is on her way to the tea-house, accompanied by her younger attendants, all of whom are portrayed in a refreshingly unsensual manner.

London, British Museum (1933–10–14–02)

EISHI (1756–1829)

18. *Party on a riverboat*

Before 1800. Detail, 27 × 43½ in (68·5 × 110·5 cm)

This must be an elaborate party organized by the
womenfolk of rich merchants. The women sit on a red
carpet eating tid-bits, while hired entertainers sing and
dance for them. The party could well be taking place on
the Sumida river, one of the most important of Edo's many
waterways. In 1800, Eishi was invited to make a painting
of this very river to be presented to a member of the
imperial family when he visited Edo, an unusual honour
for a print-maker. The painting was later shown to the
retired Emperor Sakuramachi who liked it so much he
added it to his collection. Eishi commemorated this honour
by using the signature seal 'viewed by heaven' on his
work from then on.

London, British Museum (1906–12–20–277)

TOYOKUNI (1769–1825)

19. *Bandō Mitsugorō and Segawa Rosaburō*

c.1802. 14¾ × 9½in (36·5 × 24cm)

Toyokuni, the second head of the Utagawa family, is
generally considered to be the first to launch this family
into specializing in the actor-print, but his style was
heavily influenced by such great contemporaries as
Sharaku and Shunshō, and later, even by his prolific and
dominating pupil, Kunisada. The scene in this print is one
in which a feudal lord has summoned a famous courtesan
to entertain him; a conspirator takes the opportunity to try
to assassinate him by thrusting a sword from beneath the
verandah.

London, British Museum (1909–6–18–87)

HOKUSAI (1760–1849)

20. *Bullfinch on a branch of weeping cherry*

1840s. 7 × 8in (18 × 20·5cm)

Seasons play a vital role in Japanese life; homes are decorated with seasonal flowers, and the pictures hung in the *toko no ma*, the important alcove in the best room, always reflect the season in some way. This cheerful print of a bullfinch, perched upside down on a branch of weeping cherry, is a spring picture, one of several flower-and-bird prints that Hokusai produced in his late sixties and early seventies. They would have been bought by people who could not afford to decorate their houses with hand-painted pictures. Here Hokusai has distorted the blossom to make it look larger than life, so that the bird looks small and more vulnerable.

London, British Museum (1910–6–14–29)

HOKUSAI (1760–1849)

21. *Southerly wind and fine weather*

Late 1820s 10 × 14¾in (25·5 × 37·5cm)

This print, *the Great Wave* and *Lightening over Fuji*, all from the series *Thirty-Six views of Mount Fuji*, are probably the most famous images in all Japanese art. With this series, Hokusai elevated the *nishiki-e* from its popular status to the level of high art, and liberated it from its almost exclusive preoccupation with the depiction of human beings. His genius is particularly evident in this print, which shows a breathtakingly original view of the sacred mountain, using a limited range of colours. The subject had been shown in thousands of paintings by other artists. The proportions of this print are classical; the seven to three ratio had been a tradition in Japanese art since the tenth century.

London, British Museum (1906–12–20–525)

HOKUSAI

22. *The Fields of Sekiya by the Sumida river*

1823–31. 9⅓ × 14½in (23·5 × 36·8cm)

Sekiya today is well within metropolitan Tokyo, but when Hokusai depicted it in his series, *Thirty-six views of Mount Fuji*, it was a lonely village where idle intellectuals could go to escape the city. The Sumida, one of the most important waterways of Edo, was a narrow river running through rice plantations. The mist rising from the marshland looks natural, but is, at the same time, depicted in the conventional manner. In most of the other prints in this series, with the notable exception of the masterpiece *Southerly wind and fine weather* (*plate 21*), Hokusai depicts the mountain in cool blues, greens or greys; here, however, Fuji is a reddish brown, suggesting early morning.

London, British Museum (1906–12–20–551)

SHIGENOBU (1784–1832)

23. *Scene from a* kabuki *play*

$6\frac{3}{4} \times 8in$ *(17 × 20cm)*

This actor-print by Shigenobu, Hokusai's pupil and one-time son-in-law, uses a very traditional composition, with the man standing and the woman on the ground. In almost all Japanese love stories, it is the woman who declares her love and, if necessary, pursues the man. Consequently, the man sometimes had to reject the woman forcefully, as is pictured here. The man's distinctive staff shows him to be a pilgrim.

London, British Museum (1902–2–12–377)

KUNISADA (1786–1864)

24. *Bandō Hikozaburō*

c.1850. 13¾ × 9¾ in (35 × 24·5cm)

The *kabuki* play from which this scene is taken is a typical
example of how playwrights combined several true stories
that captured the popular imagination to create a single
play. The 'Kagamiyama' plays have as their main plot the
true story of a palace revolution which threatened to
destroy one of the most powerful feudal families. The
incident of a lady-in-waiting beating a subordinate with
her slipper, however, took place in an entirely different
household. But both stories involved powerful *samurai*
families and their women, and provided juicy scandal for
the townspeople, who were considered unworthy of
knowing anything about their betters.

Cambridge, Collection the Author

KUNISADA (1786–1864)

25. *Scene from a play*

14⅝ × 10in (37·5 × 25·5cm)

Kunisada is often criticized for letting his standards drop through over-production, but most critics agree that the period during which he produced this print (when he signed himself Gototei Kunisada) was his best. Here two fishermen stand, understandably amazed, as they haul up an unusual catch, a *geisha*. Her undergarment is red, considered very erotic by the Japanese, and we have a glimpse of white thigh. This restraint contrasts with the many extremely explicit erotic prints that Kunisada produced.

London, British Museum (1907–5–31–607)

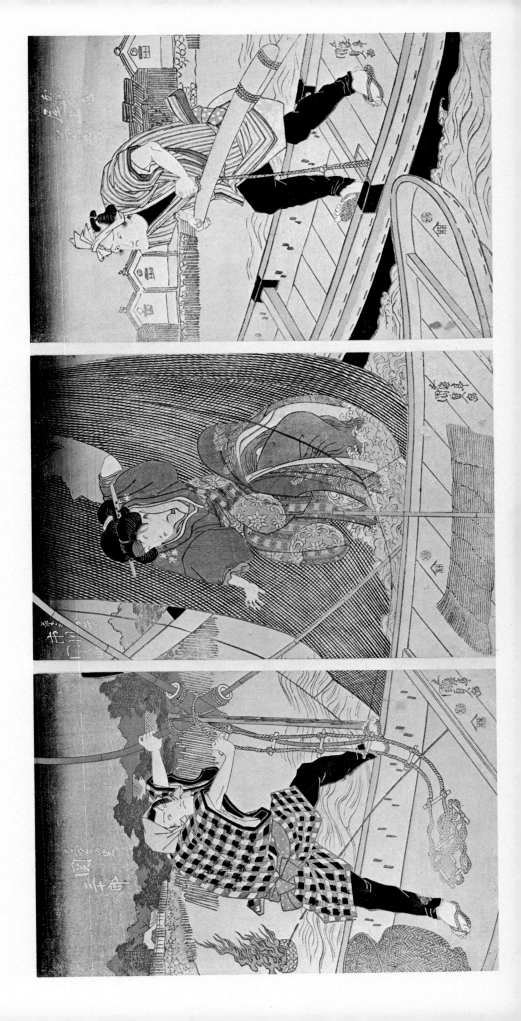

KUNISADA (1786–1864)

26. *The moon*

1857. 14⅜ × 9⅜ in (36·5 × 24 cm)

This print is one of those that demonstrate how technically perfect the wood-block had become by the mid-nineteenth century, when a variety of clear bright colours were used which had been unavailable to artists like Haronobu working a century before. According to Lawrence Binyon, who first catalogued the British Museum's collection, the triptych from which this print comes is an illustration of a scene in the great mediaeval Japanese novel, *Tale of Genji*, by Lady Murasaki. However, the woman is in contemporary dress and she could equally well be part of a merchant family preparing for a musical evening. The instrument at her feet is a *koto*.

London, British Museum (1906-12-20-1110)

KUNISADA (1786–1864)

27. *Two main characters from a* kabuki *play*

14 × 9¾in (35·5 × 25cm)

The two characters pictured here, Chogoro and Chokichi, are shown by their hair styles to be, respectively, a wrestler and a gangster. The first two words of the title of the play, *Futatsu chocho kuruwa nikki*, meaning two butterflies, is a pun on their names. The plot is a typical *kabuki* one about friendship conflicting with loyalty and love. The markings on the actors' faces are red because they are 'good'; the 'wicked' characters would have blue markings. The subtle blending of pink, highlighting the forehead and the nose, is a characteristic of *kabuki* make-up, while the way the colour has been transferred to the wood-block print is a triumph of the inker's skill.

Cambridge, Collection the Author

EISEN (1789–1848)

28. *The Kegon falls*

c.1835. 8¾ × 13½in (22 × 34·5cm)

The Kegon falls in Nikkō are the highest in Japan, and since Nikkō enshrines Tokugawa Ieyasu, the founder of the Shogunate, it was a popular pilgrimage site. Eisen's life-style was notorious even among his rough-living colleagues. He was a popular poet and playwright, who drank so much that he often forgot commissions. He ran a brothel for a while, and wrote and illustrated much homosexual pornography. Although his publishers tried to get him to design travel and landscape prints, knowing that he had been trained in one of the traditional schools, he is best known for his prints of curiously hunchbacked but sensual women. This print shows the influence of Hokusai's many experiments with the depiction of water, which, here, is not very convincing. The main attraction of this print lies in the three charming little men, fearfully peering over the cliff, who play an important part in establishing the scale of the picture. This is an *ai-e*, or blue colour print, a type which Eisen is said to have originated and which was much used by subsequent artists.

London, British Museum (1948–4–10–033)

KUNIYOSHI (1798–1861)

29. *Taisō rescuing Shōjō and Gakuwa*

1828–9. 58 × 38in (145 × 96·5cm)

Kuniyoshi was almost as prolific in his output as Kunisada, his older contemporary. Of the many subjects he tackled, his warrior-prints were the most popular, particularly the series to which this print belongs, *108 heroes of the Suikoden*, depicting heroes of the popular Chinese classic, the *Water Margin* (re-written in Japanese by Bakin). It was Kuniyoshi's first success and immediately type-cast him as a specialist in the warrior-print, which he seems not to have minded, possibly because historical prints were a convenient vehicle for criticizing the authorities. He did this by showing known contemporary figures transposed into an historical setting for the purposes of lampooning them.

London, British Museum (1906–12–20–1334)

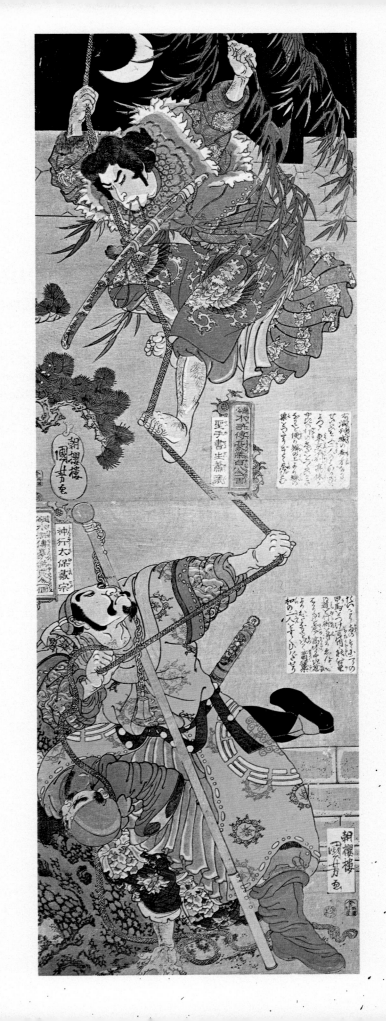

KUNIYOSHI (1798–1861)

30. *Minamato no Yoshitsune*

1851–2. Triptych, each panel 14½ × 10in (37 × 25·5cm)

This print has all the most picturesque elements of
Japanese art – a legend surrounding the youth of an
historical hero, monsters, swordplay, a variety of bright
colours and menacing shadows. Minamoto no Yoshitsune,
the brilliant twelfth-century military leader, was killed
by order of his jealous elder brother, whom he helped to
make military governor of the country. Even now he is a
popular figure in art and literature. This print shows him
as a boy, when he was hiding in the mountains near
Kyoto, preparing to overthrow the enemies of his family by
learning the martial arts from a priest. The print is full of
movement; the huge, dark, curiously soft figure of the
priest, boldly set in the middle of the tryptych, makes the
figures appear to spin around it.

London, British Museum (1907–5–31–623)

KUNIYOSHI (1798–1861)

31. *Mt. Fuji seen from the banks of the Sumida river*

1842. 10¼ × 15¼ in (26 × 38·5cm)

The success of Hokusai and Hiroshige's travel landscapes caused many publishers to commission their artists to work on similar themes. This print is a fine example of the versatility of Kuniyoshi, who could turn his hand successfully to almost any subject. There is considerable Western influence in the shading of the river bank. Kuniyoshi was, like many of his contemporaries, extremely curious about the West, and produced many prints in the Western style. These are, at best, experiments in methods which appear strange to the Westerner, but once the technique was mastered and incorporated into familiar subjects, it became a great asset to this artist.

U.K., Private Collection

HIROSHIGE (1797–1858)

32. *Goyu, on the Tōkaidō*

1833–4. 15⅕ × 10⅓ in (38·5 × 26cm)

Hisaka in the Sayo mountains

1833–4. 15⅕ × 10⅓ in (38·5 × 26cm)

The Tōkaidō was the highway between Kyoto and Edo (now Tokyo); his series depicting it was Hiroshige's first success, completed when he was 37 years old, and from then on his prints remained popular until he died. This inevitably resulted in his being forced to over-produce, and in publishers commissioning him to go into co-production with other popular artists like Kunisada and Eisen. These gimmicks seldom worked, and there are some very inferior prints bearing Hiroshige's signature. Hokusai had already published four series on the Tōkaidō, but Hiroshige's prints had a peculiar freshness, perhaps because he made all the sketches while travelling the route in the party of a feudal lord. In the print above, two travellers are being dragged into one of the inns by serving maids, where one of their earlier victims is having his feet washed. The young woman by the window is a prostitute, attached to the inn, whose lack of interest in proceedings show her to be already booked for the night.

The other print is from the same series. The Hisaka station was neither as beautiful, nor was the road there as steep as this print suggests. Hiroshige had a sentimental streak which appealed to his public; the large stone at which the travellers are gazing was said to have been on the spot where a pregnant woman, going over the mountains to meet her husband, was killed by a bandit. She clung, dying, to the stone. The goddess of mercy took pity on her, so that when the child was removed from her body after her death, it survived.

London, British Museum (1906–12–20–805 and 1906–12–20–775)

HIROSHIGE (1797–1858)

33. *Maple leaves at the Tekona shrine, Mamma*

1857. 13¾ × 9⅖in (35 × 24cm)

This print comes from Hiroshige's last great series, *One hundred views of Edo*. He died before it could be completed, and his son-in-law and successor, Hiroshige II, has his signature on three of the prints. Hiroshige experimented successfully in this series with the device of bringing part of the scenery well into the foreground. He has an eagle hovering over an aerial view of Fukagawa; lengths of dyed cloth wave in the wind to the right of a print of Kanda; Whistler took the idea for his *Battersea Bridge* from an under-bridge view of Tsukuda. Here, we are invited to look at the scenery through bright, red maple leaves, a photographic composition by an artist who had no knowledge of photography. This series came out four years after the arrival of the first Westerners in Japan, and was brought into Europe almost immediately. Whistler was not the only artist to be inspired by the prints; Vincent van Gogh faithfully copied two of them.

London, British Museum (1906–12–20–652)

GAKUTEI (active 1820–45)

34. *Sudden rain on Mt. Tempō*

1834. 14⅞ × 10in (38 × 25·5cm)

Gakutei, like Eisen, was influenced by Hokusai's and
Hiroshige's treatment of water and rain. The foam on the
crest of the waves is not very convincing, but the blurred
edges of the storm clouds and the very fine lines of the rain
point to skilled cutters and inkers on the production team.
The rather superfluous white patch framing the bottom of
the picture is a concession to the tradition of framing
paintings liberally with white, gold, or silver 'mist'. This
print is from Gakutei's most successful series about Mt.
Tempō, the artificial hill which was built in 1831 at the
mouth of the Aji river in Osaka. The area around it
became a kind of picnic ground for the inhabitants of the
city.

London, British Museum (1931–4–27–010)

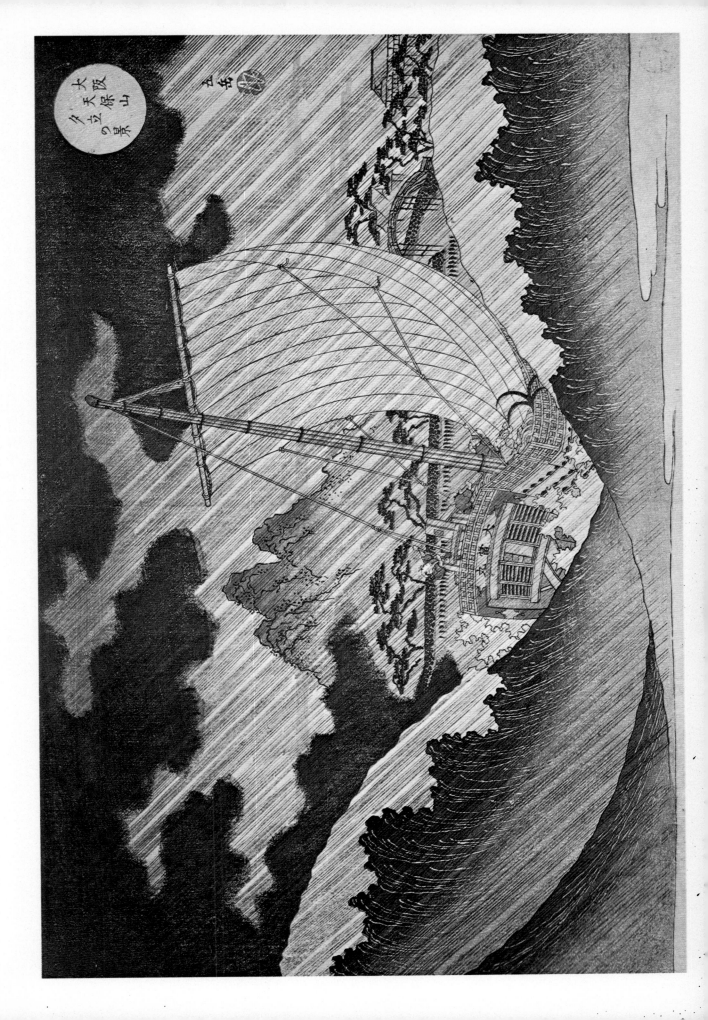

KUNICHIKA (1835–1900)

35. *Portrait of Nakamura Shikan IV as Ishikawa Hachiemon*

1869. 13⅞ × 9⅝in (35 × 24·5cm)

Kunichika, a pupil of Kunisada, is generally considered to be the last truly traditional *ukiyo-e* artist. He did not bother with the 'modern' themes that became popular after the opening up of Japan to the world, but concentrated on the *kabuki*, which continued to attract crowds in spite of the influx of Western plays. He prided himself on living in the 'Edo' manner, lavishly and not worrying about tomorrow. He had many pupils, worked through some forty wives, and moved house sixty-four times.

London, British Museum (1906–12–20–1132)

KUNITERU II
36. *Shimbashi station*
1871. 14 × 9¼in (35·5 × 23·5cm)

Kuniteru was a pupil of Kunisada, who did his best work
in depicting the new and exciting happenings of the early
years of the Meiji restoration. This print of Shimbashi, the
first Tokyo railway station, must have been made in 1871,
when the inaugural train left for Yokohama. The event
took on the proportions of a national celebration, and was
commemorated in countless prints depicting the scene
from every conceivable angle. Although there is a word for
station in the Japanese language, a railway station was
called *sutensho* or *suteiishon*, one of the first English words
to get into everyday Japanese usage, albeit in a distorted
form.

Cambridge, Collection Dr. John McMaster

YOSHITAKI (1840–1899)

37. *Leading members of the government discuss the invasion of Korea*

1877. Triptych, each panel 14 × 9½in (35·5 × 24cm)

The *Seikanron* was a contentious issue which plagued the Meiji government from the start, and finally led to the revolt and suicide of Saigō Takamori (gesturing in the centre) and his followers. Saigō Takamori wished to invade Korea to break her isolation, because, amongst other things, a war would unite the restless ex-*samurai* in a common cause. This is a good example of the typical Meiji print, with strong colours and a mixture of costumes, Western and Japanese. But Yoshitaki, an artist who worked in Osaka, appears to have produced this one in a hurry, with little imagination and less attempt at portraiture, with the result that all the men look much alike.

Cambridge, Collection Dr. John McMaster

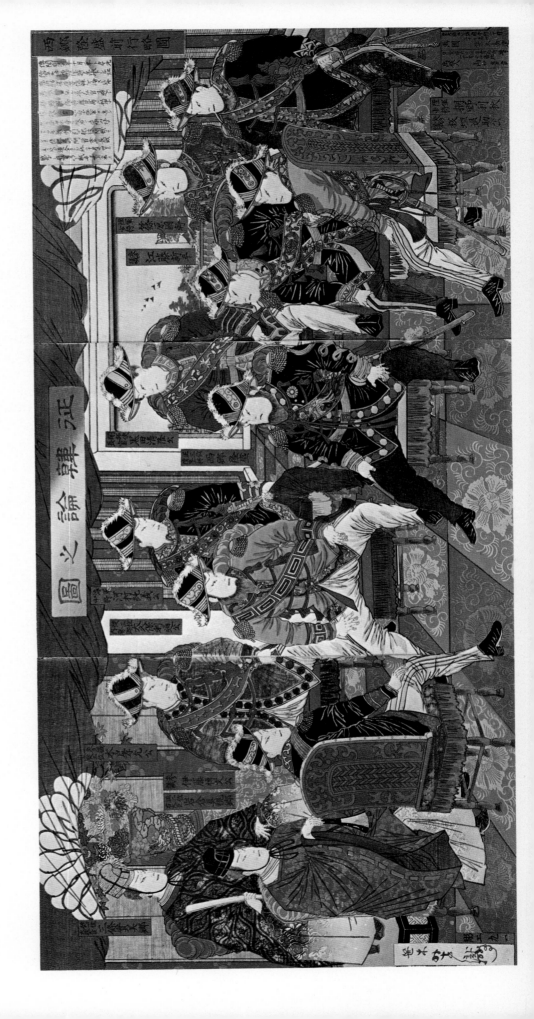

HIROSHIGE III (1841–1894)

38. *The stone bridge at Edobashi*

14 × 9in (35·5 × 23cm)

Hiroshige III succeeded to the name on marrying the master's daughter, after she divorced her first husband, who had been called Hiroshige II. His output was enormous, his subjects consisting mostly of scenes showing the rapid changes in the country brought on by Western influence. Stone was used very seldom for Japanese traditional buildings, and brick was almost unknown, a sensible omission since Tokyo is a very earthquake-prone city. Still, until most of the brick buildings and stone bridges collapsed in the catastrophic quake of 1923, they were the proud manifestations of Japan's modernization.

Cambridge, Collection Dr. John McMaster

SHŌGETSU

39. *The honourable place of handicrafts in education*

1890. $14\frac{1}{2} \times 9\frac{1}{2}$ in (37 × 24cm)

This is an excellent example of the Meiji print, with the garish aniline dyes and the outlandish mixture of Japanese faces and Western dress, Japanese house and Western furniture. But Shōgetsu's draughtsmanship and the sureness of the block cutter's chisel show a high level of craftsmanship, rare at this late date. Note the delightful sewing machine, enshrined in the centre; it is the most modern thing in the print and is given pride of place.

Cambridge, Collection Dr. John McMaster

TOSHIYOSHI

40. 'Terrible war of General Sakamoto . . .'

1894. Triptych, each panel 14 × 9½ in (35·5 × 24cm)

On 17 September, 1894, during the battle of the Yellow Sea, the Japanese gunboat *Akagi* came under heavy fire from three Chinese battleships which surrounded her. The *Akagi* managed to stay afloat, but her commander, General Sakamoto, was killed, as were many of his men. The Sino-Japanese War was the first test of the Japanese armed strength against a foreign enemy, and was also very useful for the new government in that it united the various factions within the country. Japan's victory after nine months resulted in the formal acquisition of Korea and Formosa as colonies, and for the first time, a feeling of superiority over the Chinese, which had never existed before.

Cambridge, Collection Dr. John McMaster

CECILIA WHITFORD AND BLACKER CALMANN COOPER LIMITED would like to thank the following for allowing works in their collections to be reproduced: the Cambridge University Library (plate 2) and Dr. John McMaster (plates 36–40). Plates 1, 3–23, 25, 26, 28–30 and 32–35 are reproduced by permission of the Trustees of the British Museum. The transparency for plate 31 was provided by the Cooper-Bridgeman Library. They are also indebted to Mr. L. Smith of the Department of Oriental Antiquities, British Museum, for his assistance in research.